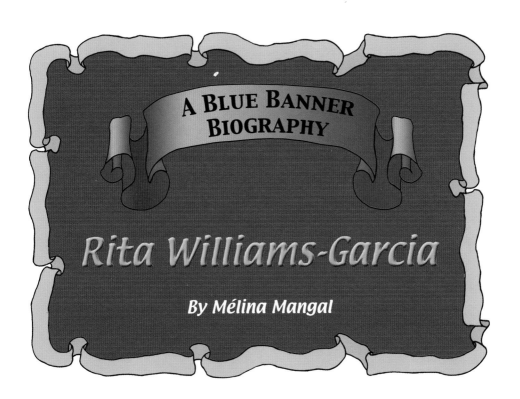

A BLUE BANNER BIOGRAPHY

Rita Williams-Garcia

By Mélina Mangal

Mitchell Lane
PUBLISHERS

P.O. Box 196
Hockessin, Delaware 19707
Visit us on the web: www.mitchelllane.com
Comments? email us: mitchelllane@mitchelllane.com

Printing   1   2   3   4   5   6   7   8   9

Blue Banner Biographies

Eminem	Sally Field	Jodie Foster
Melissa Gilbert	Rudy Giuliani	Ron Howard
Michael Jackson	Nelly	Mary-Kate and Ashley Olsen
Daniel Radcliffe	Shirley Temple	Ritchie Valens
Rita Williams-Garcia		

Library of Congress Cataloging-in-Publication Data
Mangal, Mélina.
      Rita Williams-Garcia / Melina Mangal.
         p. cm. — (A Blue banner biography)
Summary: Discusses the life and career of Rita Williams-Garcia, award-winning African-American
    author of books for children and young adults.
Includes bibliographical references and index.
      ISBN 1-58415-217-6 (Library Bound)
      1. Williams-Garcia, Rita—Juvenile literature. 2. Authors, American—20th century—Biogra-
phy—Juvenile literature. 3. African American authors—Biography—Juvenile literature. 4.
Children's stories—Authorship—Juvenile literature. [1. Williams-Garcia, Rita. 2. Authors,
American. 3. African Americans—Biography. 4. Women—Biography.] I. Title. II. Series.
      PS3545.I5473Z77 2003
      813'.54--dc21
                                   2003000681

ABOUT THE AUTHOR: Mélina Mangal received her Master's of Science in Library Science from the University of North Carolina at Chapel Hill, and holds Bachelor's degrees in Business Administration and French. Her works of fiction and non-fiction appear in various anthologies. She also works as a school media specialist in Minnesota, where she lives with her husband.

PHOTO CREDITS: All photos courtesy Rita Williams-Garcia, except page 4, photographed by Peter Garcia, courtesy of Random House.

ACKNOWLEDGMENTS: Special thanks to Rita Williams-Garcia, who graciously provided information during telephone interviews in the fall of 2002.

2-12-04

CONTENTS

Rita's work wasn't published by the first publisher she wrote to. It took years of perseverance for Rita to become the accomplished writer she is today.

Holding On to a Dream

Rita Williams-Garcia knows about patience and perseverance. Despite many obstacles, she held on to her dream of writing.

One day in 1985, Rita Williams-Garcia received bad news. The marketing company she worked for was sold. Rita lost her job as a promotional writer. She had to decide if she should go back to working in the mailroom, as she had years before, or if she should be the writer she'd dreamed of being.

Rita pulled an old manuscript from under her bed. Although she had already sent it out years earlier, no publishers had accepted it. The rejection letters said Rita's character, Joyce, was not a good role model. They said readers wouldn't understand Rita's references to black culture. Rita proved them wrong. She became the writer she was meant to be.

"I took out my draft of *Blue Tights* and thought about how I would revise and sell it," Rita wrote years later. She found six publishers in *The Writer's Market*, and one of them, Lodestar, accepted her story. *Blue Tights* was published in 1988.

After her first book came more, all of them with strong characters. Some of Rita's characters try to fit in, others try to figure themselves out. All of them are memorable.

> **Some of Rita's characters try to fit in, others try to figure themselves out. All of them are memorable.**

Some of Rita's stories deal with difficult subjects, like teen pregnancy or rape, because Rita believes it is important to show the real lives of real people. "I just try to be honest," she said about dealing with stark subjects. "Once you shed the light in the dark places, they're less frightening."

But some critics find Rita's work too graphic. Rita's third book, *Like Sisters on the Homefront,* was removed from several different schools because some adults thought the language in it was too explicit. But the truthfulness of Rita's story triumphed. *Like Sisters on the Homefront* won the *Booklist* Editor's Choice Award and was named a Coretta Scott King Honor Book.

Rita's second book, *Fast Talk on a Slow Track,* also won numerous awards, including the Parents' Choice

Award. Despite the obstacles presented by publishers and censors, Rita pursued her dream of highlighting young people whose stories haven't been told. She knew she was on the right track when she received a letter from a veteran teacher in Texas. Rita's book made her feel something she had not felt in all her years of teaching. It had given her a fresh perspective. "It was a rewarding feeling to know I'd opened something up," Rita said of the teacher's feelings.

This is the story of how Rita overcame many obstacles to open up the minds and hearts of many more readers.

Despite obstacles, Rita pursued her dream of highlighting young people whose stories haven't been told.

The Early Days

On April 13, 1957, Rita Williams was born in Jamaica, Queens, New York. Rita's mother was so tired after her birth that her cousin, Virginia, a pediatric nurse, named her.

"We were your typical black family," says Rita. "My parents worked hard and instilled strong values, like education and family." Rita's father, James Jasper "Russell" Williams, was born in Williamston, North Carolina, but grew up in New York. Like many African Americans who moved from the segregated South to the North in search of a better life, six-year-old James moved to New York with his mother, Edith Williams, and his younger brother, Clayton. When James was a teenager, he became a Golden Glove boxer and competed in many fights.

Rita's father, James Jasper "Russell" Williams, was a Golden Glove contender when he was seventeen years old.

Rita's mother, Magdalene Coston, known as Essie Mae, was born in Smithville, Virginia, near Norfolk. Her brothers had already left home as men by that time. They had learned the Navajo language during military training in Arizona and had become Code Talkers (people trained to talk in code to avoid being overheard by the enemy) during World War II.

James David Coston, Essie Mae's father, was a successful landscaper. In his spare time he worked on projects at the Hampton Institute, an historically black institution for higher learning. His example influenced both Essie Mae and, later, Rita. He would often go to the courthouse and ask a judge to turn over a troubled youth to him. Then he would show that young man how to complete projects. "Hard work will make a man of him," he'd say.

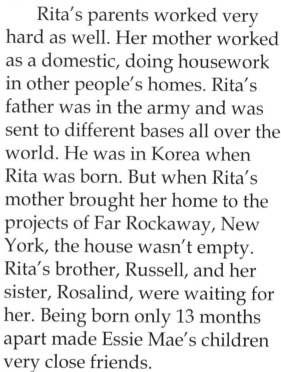

During the day when Essie Mae left for work, Rita would play with her brother and sister.

Rita's parents worked very hard as well. Her mother worked as a domestic, doing housework in other people's homes. Rita's father was in the army and was sent to different bases all over the world. He was in Korea when Rita was born. But when Rita's mother brought her home to the projects of Far Rockaway, New York, the house wasn't empty. Rita's brother, Russell, and her sister, Rosalind, were waiting for her. Being born only 13 months apart made Essie Mae's children very close friends.

During the day Essie Mae would leave her children at home while she went to work. Rita would play all day with her brother and sister. "We were all each other's best friends," Rita remembered. They had a pet unlike any other, a cockroach named Stanley. Rita's mother didn't think it was much of a pet and threw it out.

One day in the kitchen, Rosalind and Russell hoisted their little sister onto the counter. "We made

Rita's godmother, Virginia Robinson (shown here), gave Rita her name and often visited Rita, her brother Russell, and her sister Rosalind.

snow from the flour and sugar crystals. I got into the peanut butter, and then Mom walked in," Rita recounted. Since food was hard to come by in those days, her mother was not pleased.

When the army transferred Rita's father to Fort Ord, near Seaside, California, the Williams family traveled all the way across the country. Rita was only three years old, but she remembered that long car trip. When the family stopped in Arizona, there were plenty of new sights and sounds. "We saw mountain lions, horned toads, snakes, Pueblo Indians selling moccasins, dolls and turquoise jewelry by the roadside, alcoholic cowboys, and a blanket of stars almost every night."

At night, as her family slept in their car, Rita heard wildcats in the mountains. It was both exciting and terrifying. Even more terrifying for young Rita, however, was the way her family's car was stopped by police one day in Arizona. The nervous and frightened reaction of her mother left a lasting impression on Rita. In those days it was difficult for African Americans to find a place to spend the night because of segregation laws. These laws made it illegal for African Americans to use the same facilities as whites to eat, work, travel, or study. Everything was separate.

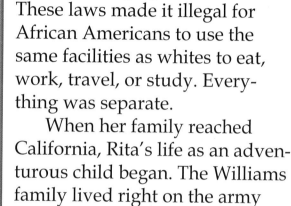

Rita and her siblings would pile all their toys under a mattress to make an indoor slide.

When her family reached California, Rita's life as an adventurous child began. The Williams family lived right on the army base and had a large backyard. "It was a magical place for me," Rita said. She could see the stars at night, and they seemed very close in the vast dark sky.

Rosalind, Russell, and Rita played all kinds of games together. They would pile all their toys under a mattress to make an indoor slide. They would play dodgeball and kickball. Sometimes they would have little wars, pretending that clods of dirt were exploding bombs. They also enjoyed roller-skating and raiding plum trees.

But Rita also like to read. "I learned to read at age two by looking at billboards, figuring out the sounds

Rita was reading and writing many different stories by the time she was in third grade.

associated with the letters and putting it all together," she said in an interview. When Rosalind was in kindergarten, she would slide books into Rita's playpen and listen while Rita read the story to her. "I had to make up some of the words, but many I figured out," she wrote later.

Rita was attracted to words from the very beginning. "The first words that truly fascinated me were homonyms. I actually recall being in my playpen, playing with the different meanings for *lone, alone, loan,* and *bologna,* and *see, sea, C.* It kept me amused for hours!"

Reading kept Rita occupied and fascinated with the world, but as she grew older, she yearned for good books about black people. By sixth grade she had read and reread every book in her school library that featured a black person, like the biographies of Sojourner Truth, Booker T. Washington, and Harriet Tubman.

While Rita's father was away fighting in the Vietnam War, Rita wrote him many letters.

Rita asked for more books with black female characters. The librarian located several stories about a young, adventurous West African girl. In *Thirty-One Brothers and Sisters* and *Nomusa and the New Magic,* Rita found excitement and an intelligent tomboy character that looked and acted like her. As she recalled, "It was my first trip to Africa!" Those books gave her positive images of Africa. They helped erase from her mind the negative way Africans were shown on American television in those days.

Rita's father was sent to fight in the Vietnam War in 1967. While he was away, Rita wrote him many letters. She also watched the news every night and heard about the heavy bombing and violent attacks that killed many people in Vietnam. "We were terrified, but we tried to be brave," Rita said years later.

One day two army officers knocked on their door with bad news. Rita's father's unit had been bombed. Fortunately, he was alive in a field hospital. Although his shoulder was injured, he would be fine after a while. He went back into battle after that, and returned home in 1968.

Rita was so happy to have her father back alive. He visited her classroom one day, wearing his dress uniform. His polished shoes and war decorations shone. As he answered her classmates' questions, Rita could barely contain her excitement and pride. She ended up asking more questions than anyone else!

With the return of Rita's father came big changes. Many children with parents in the military are used to moving, but Rita's family had been in California for almost 10 years. In 1969, Rita's father was sent to Fort Benning, Georgia, where his family joined him after several months. Six months later Rita's father was out of the army and the family moved back to New York to live with Rita's grandmother Edith. Rita's life was about to change forever.

Many children with parents in the military are used to moving, but Rita's family had been in California for almost 10 years.

A Writer is Born

*R*ita started writing around the age of four. She wrote rhyming poetry and adventure stories that featured her sister, brother, and herself. So much was happening in the world around her at that time: the assassinations of John F. Kennedy, Robert Kennedy, Martin Luther King Jr., and Malcolm X; the Vietnam War; anti-war protests; and civil rights demonstrations. "I watched the news and read the paper, filling my stories with floods, tornadoes, bombings, riots, and stern faces of white men surrounded by red, white, and blue banners running from the president," Rita wrote of her first stories.

"The librarian also gave me Louise Fitzhugh's *Harriet the Spy*, which encouraged me to keep a journal." From then on, Rita wrote in her notebook.

Leaving California had been difficult for Rita. "I was thrown into culture shock," she wrote about the move. But the change got her writing. When she was 12, Rita wrote a novel about her life in California.

Life in New York was rough. Rita had to deal with being poor. When her father left the army, he had lost his source of income. Rita went to school with old clothes and holes in her shoes. Students at school noticed. "I took a bright pink Band-Aid and put it on and just kept walking," Rita said about covering a hole in her shoe. "I didn't care. I wanted to be different."

Rita's first story was published by Highlights *magazine when she was fourteen years old.*

Rita liked being an individual and didn't want to change. "I was a proud little nerd with my hands clasped on my desk ready to rocket in the air when the teacher asked a question. My classmates wanted to kill me," she wrote about being in a new school. Others picked fights with her because she wouldn't conform. Luckily, Rita had her writing. "My best friend was my notebook," she said.

> *Rita saw herself as strong and proud, not wanting to be involved with all the fighting around her.*

Life was also tough at home. Rita's father, a wounded Vietnam veteran, was dealing with horrifying war memories, and Rita's mother had become an independent woman who wanted to change the world. Her parents began fighting every day. Rita escaped into books. As she wrote years later, "I mostly read anything by Nikki Giovanni, Angela Davis, Bobby Seale, Huey Newton, and lots of Shakespeare." She also wrote one thousand words a day and began sending her stories to publishers. Rita had many stories to tell.

One day at school there was a lockdown because a seventh-grader killed another student with a butcher knife. While waiting in a room with a few tough girls, Rita wrote a story about a strong girl who didn't have to beat anyone down to be herself. That's how she saw herself: strong and proud, not wanting to be involved with all the fighting around her.

Writing kept Rita going. She studied *The Writer's Market, Literary Market Place,* and *The Writer's Handbook* at the public library. There she found information about publishers and where to send her stories. She would type the stories on her sister's manual typewriter, then mail them out. Each day she would rush home from school to see if a letter had arrived from a publisher. Most of the mail she received was rejection letters, but that didn't stop her. She was happy to get letters recognizing her as a writer.

Rita didn't just write about what she saw around her. She also traveled in her stories. Based on what she heard from her Filipino friend Corazon, she was inspired to write a story called "Ben-ji Speaks." About a young boy in the Philippines who discovers a way to talk to birds, "Ben-ji Speaks" became Rita's first published story. When Rita was 14, *Highlights* magazine bought it for publication. Rita was now a published author.

> *Rita didn't mind receiving rejection letters from publishers, since they recognized her as a writer.*

From *Blue Tights* to *Rainbows*

*T*here were so many other happenings in her life that Rita didn't actively pursue writing as a career until much later. In 1972, Rita's family moved from her grandmother's house in St. Albans to their own in Jamaica, Queens, New York. In 1973, Rita's family went on welfare. Rita was so angry and ashamed, she went out and found a job. At 16 she started working at a Haitian restaurant owned by the mother of her friend Jeanine. Rita would walk 31 blocks from Jamaica to the restaurant in Cambria Heights. After work she would bring plates of food home, which helped her family during the toughest times. "[Jeanine's] mother made sure we ate over the summer," Rita said of her employer.

Rita kept writing while at Benjamin N. Cardozo High School in Bayside, but by the time she graduated, a new love had come into her life: dance. "I had a gift for dance but was too shy to pursue it in high school," she wrote. As soon as she enrolled at Hofstra University in Hempstead, New York, she began taking dance classes. "I lived in leotards," she wrote of her college days. Rita would jump on the train after classes at Hofstra on Long Island to study dance at the renowned Alvin Ailey dance studio in midtown Manhattan, and also at Phil Black's in Manhattan.

Rita fell in love with dance when she was in high school.

Although economics was her major, Rita spent much of her time dancing. She loved the energetic, soulful, and spiritual movement she learned at Alvin Ailey's. She was so captivated by dance that she dreamed of inventing her own movements. "I wanted to create my own dance language," she said of those times. "The choreographer in me wanted to tell a story." She even formed her own dance troupe, Miles Per Minute.

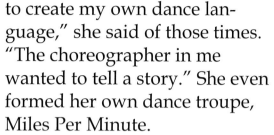

Rita tutored teenage girls for a sorority project as part of a community outreach literacy program.

Rita wasn't writing as much as she had before because of classes, dance, and her involvement in Alpha Kappa Alpha, the oldest African-American national sorority, founded in 1908. But it was actually a sorority project that got her back into writing. Rita tutored teenage girls as part of a community outreach literacy program. When she couldn't find stories the girls could relate to, Rita wrote character sketches and short scenes that her students acted out. They couldn't wait for more. So Rita wrote more.

By this time Rita had changed her major to liberal arts and was taking a fiction workshop with well-known writers Sonia Pilcer and Richard Price. They encouraged her to work on the sketches. These sketches became the first draft of Rita's first novel, *Blue Tights.*

Rita married Peter Garcia in 1983.

Before completing her college coursework, Rita found a clerical job at a marketing company. It was perfect for her because she didn't need to dress up and could run off to auditions for shows like *The Wiz* and *Sophisticated Ladies*. Since she worked in the mailroom, the company allowed Rita to use the office typewriter, make photocopies, and mail out her manuscripts.

But the competition of dance auditions required at least four hours of dancing a day. Because of her job, Rita was no longer able to practice that many hours. During the late 1970s and early 1980s, AIDS erupted into the dance world. Many of Rita's friends and acquaintances on Broadway were dying of the mysterious disease. It became painful for Rita to remain in that environment.

To make matters worse, Rita received more rejection letters from publishers. "After three years of trying to sell it, I threw it under my bed, never to be seen again," Rita said of *Blue Tights.* She decided to focus on her marketing job.

Life got better when Rita married Peter Garcia in 1983. She was working as a promotional writer at the same marketing company, but she was not doing much of her own writing, and she wasn't dancing. A year later Rita gave birth to her daughter Michelle.

Rita and her first daughter Michelle. Before Michelle was born and while she was still young, Rita didn't write or dance very much.

Rita received her master's degree from Queens College in 1997.

After Rita's marketing job was eliminated, she completed work for her college degree. In 1987 Rita graduated from Hofstra University. That's also when she got back to her own writing. Almost nine years after starting her first sketches, Rita published her first book.

Later in 1988 Rita gave birth to her second daughter, Stephanie. And she kept writing. She went back to school to get a master's degree in creative writing, and she went back to work. "I can't tell you how I balanced writing, my job, school and family," Rita wrote. But she did. Her book about a young, college-bound African-American man, *Fast Talk on a Slow Track,* was published in 1991.

Like Sisters on the Homefront, about a teen mother, was published in 1995. Rita graduated from Queens College in 1997 with her master's degree. She also divorced Peter, but she kept writing. Her first picture book, *Catching the Wild Waiyuuzee,* was published in 2000. *Every Time a Rainbow Dies,* about a 16-year-old boy who falls in love with a rape victim, was published in 2001. Meanwhile Rita has had many short stories published, such as "Chalkman," about children who make a game of the chalk outline of a dead body. The many voices of Rita's characters were now being heard and felt around the world.

The many voices of Rita's characters were now being heard and felt around the world.

Life After the Rainbow

*A*lthough ideas are always dancing through Rita's head, she won't write a story until a character's voice is clear. By then, she'll already have a story plotted in her mind. Rita uses ideas from her own life, but she also explores new territory. She took "The Special," the bus Joyce takes in *Blue Tights,* to her own dance classes while in college. Many of the thoughts and feelings Joyce expresses came from Rita's own experiences as a young woman wanting to dance. *Every Time a Rainbow Dies* was born out of Rita's experience working in her friend's Haitian restaurant and from her interest in cultures of the Caribbean. As Rita said in an interview, "I hope that's the reason why we write: to go places we've never gone yet."

Rita plans on going many more places, in her writing and in her own life. She reads her work to young

Rita enjoys spending time with her daughters. Shown here are Michelle and Stephanie.

people and conducts workshops for teens. She dreams of traveling and learning more about how to make films. In 2002, Rita and an actress friend, Rashamella Cumbo, made an independent film production of her book *Every Time a Rainbow Dies*. Although the film was not released for general viewing, Rita learned a lot in the process.

Rita now works as a manager of a software distribution company, but she makes time for writing and for her daughters. She plays volleyball and loves to watch football. "I watched football with my father since I was six," she said. "I am a football fanatic." Her favorite team is the New York Jets. "I am going to be a Jets fan until I die," she confessed.

Music is another love of Rita's, even though she no longer has time to dance. She experienced the beginnings of hip-hop, with people like Kurtis Blow and members of Run DMC living in her neighborhood. She is also interested in strong people like Queen Latifah. Perhaps one day readers will get a chance to read a Rita Williams-Garcia book about Queen Latifah or someone like her—a positive and realistic role model for young African-American women. As long as Rita keeps listening to the strong voices in and around her, readers everywhere will be inspired and will keep turning page after page.

> *Music is another love of Rita's, even though she no longer has time to dance.*

1957	born on April 13 in Jamaica, Queens, New York
1960	family moves to Fort Ord in Seaside, California
1967	father is sent to fight in Vietnam War and is wounded
1968	father returns home
1969	family moves to Fort Benning, Georgia, then to St. Alban's, Queens, to live with grandmother; writes a novel about her life in California
1970	attends Linden Junior High (Junior High School 192)
1971	first story, "Ben-ji Speaks," is published by *Highlights for Children*
1972	family moves out of grandmother's house in St. Alban's to Jamaica, Queens
1975	graduates from Benjamin N. Cardozo High School in Bayside, New York; begins attending Hofstra University in Hempstead, New York; enrolls in dance classes with Alvin Ailey and Phil Black in Manhattan
1979	takes fiction workshop with Richard Price and Sonia Pilcer; tutors high school girls through sorority literacy outreach program
1983	marries Peter Garcia
1984	first daughter, Michelle, born on December 20
1987	graduates from Hofstra University
1988	first book, *Blue Tights,* is published by Lodestar; daughter Stephanie is born on October 3
1990	husband Peter sent to Saudi Arabia to fight in Persian Gulf War
1991	*Fast Talk on a Slow Track* is published; receives ALA Notable Books for Children and Young Adults citation, ALA Quick Pick for Reluctant Young Adult Readers, PEN/Norma Klein Citation for Children's Literature, and Parent's Choice Honor for Storytelling
1995	*Like Sisters on the Homefront* is published; receives Coretta Scott King Honor
1997	graduates with master's in English from Queens College; divorces Peter Garcia
2001	*Every Time a Rainbow Dies* is published
2002	produces independent film version of *Every Time a Rainbow Dies*
2003	Allen Speaker at the NCTE Conference; *No Laughter Here* published

Author's telephone interviews with Rita Williams-Garcia, fall of 2002

Something about the author: Rita Williams-Garcia
http://www.uni-giessen.de/anglistik/tefl/seminarP/mcyal98/ftAuthor.html

Learning about Rita Williams-Garcia
http://www.scils.rutgers.edu/~kvander/williamsgarcia.html

Teachers @ Random: Authors/Illustrators: Rita Williams-Garcia
http://www.randomhouse.com/teachers/authors/will.html

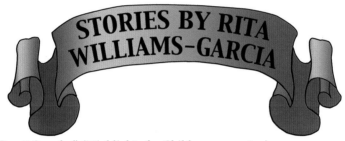

1971   "Ben-ji Speaks" (*Highlights for Children* magazine)
1988   *Blue Tights*
1991   *Fast Talk on a Slow Track*
1995   *Like Sisters on the Homefront*
          "Into the Game" (*Join In: Multiethnic Short Stories by Outstanding Writers for Young Adults*)
1997   "Chalkman" (*Twelve Shots: Outstanding Stories About Guns*)
1998   "Crazy as a Daisy" (*Stay True: Short Stories for Strong Girls*)
          "About Russell" (*Dirty Laundry*)
1999   "Clay" (*Second Sight: Stories for a New Millennium*)
          "Food From the Outside" (*When I Was Your Age: Original Stories About Growing Up, Volume 2*)
          "Wishing It Away" (*No Easy Answers: Short Stories About Teenagers Making Tough Choices*)
          "Cross Over" (*Trapped!: Cages of Mind and Body*)
2000   *Catching the Wild Waiyuuzee*
2001   *Every Time a Rainbow Dies*
2003   *No Laughter Here*

INDEX